CORPORATE SOCIAL RESPONSIBILITY AND DEVELOPMENT

VOLUME 2, ISSUE 2 OF BRILLOPEDIA

K. SANJANA

Copyright © K. Sanjana
All Rights Reserved.

This book has been published with all efforts taken to make the material error-free after the consent of the author. However, the author and the publisher do not assume and hereby disclaim any liability to any party for any loss, damage, or disruption caused by errors or omissions, whether such errors or omissions result from negligence, accident, or any other cause.

While every effort has been made to avoid any mistake or omission, this publication is being sold on the condition and understanding that neither the author nor the publishers or printers would be liable in any manner to any person by reason of any mistake or omission in this publication or for any action taken or omitted to be taken or advice rendered or accepted on the basis of this work. For any defect in printing or binding the publishers will be liable only to replace the defective copy by another copy of this work then available.

Contents

Preface

"Start writing, no matter what. The water does not flow until the faucet is turned on".

-Louis L'Amour

Hundreds of students and professors are contributing their work to Brillopedia, we are here to provide ample information about Law and Contemporary issues. Our aim is to provide a platform for today's generation to express their views and ideas on law and contemporary law

Author

CHAPTER ONE

ABSTRACT

India is the only nation who has created a mandate on the corporate to conduct some activities or to show its responsibility towards the society and it is known as Corporate Social Responsibility. Although the concept is not new, CSR has been introduced by the parliament in the amendment of 2013, Companies Act. In this paper, we will be discussing the evolution of CSR in India and it's the previous and current situation and applicability.

While discussing Corporate Social Responsibility, we will be discussing its history, principal legislation, rules and recent amendments relating to CSR. Businesses can invest their profits in areas such as education, poverty, gender equality, and hunger as part of any CSR compliance.

The type of research done here is basic, explanatory, deductive using the qualitative, secondary, descriptive data. The reason behind conducting basic, explanatory, deductive research is that the topic of research is not new and people have a considerable idea about the topic but what is the exact situation of CSR, many people don't know about the same.

The data which has been used is reliable because it has been taken from government resources. Research data is secondary, qualitative and descriptive because it is not collected by the researcher and talks about the topic in a more detailed manner. The researcher aims to conduct analytical research on the topic by analyzing the law, policies and current trends related to corporate social responsibility in India.

Over the years Corporate Social Responsibility (CSR), a concept comparatively new to India, is rapidly picking up pace. CSR has become a fundamental business practice and has gained much attention from the management of large international companies. It facilitates the alignment of business operations with social values. CSR is deemed as a point of convergence of various initiatives aimed at ensuring socio-economic development of the community. Acknowledging the fact that mainstreaming CSR into businesses could be instrumental in delivering societal value, especially in a developing country like India, this paper specifically aims at providing an understanding of concept of CSR and analyses the development of CSR in India. It highlights the policies governing CSR in India and discusses the cases of CSR initiatives in Indian firms including SMEs role in CSR. There are several challenges facing CSR in India and the paper provides suggestions to overcome them and accelerate the CSR initiatives in India.

Keywords: Corporate social responsibility, CSR initiatives, CSR Challenges

CHAPTER TWO

INTRODUCTION

AN ANALYSIS OF CORPORATE SOCIAL RESPONSIBILITY IN INDIA "A company should have in its DNA, a sense to work for the welfare of the community. CSR is an extension of individual sense of social responsibility. Active participation in CSR projects is important for a company" - Ratan Tata

The concept of corporate social responsibility has gained prominence from all avenues. The present societal marketing concept of companies is constantly evolving and has given rise to a new concept-Corporate Social Responsibility. Many of the leading corporations across the world had realized the importance of being associated with socially relevant causes as a means of promoting their brands. It stems from the desire to do well and get self satisfaction in return as well as societal obligation of business. As an engine for social progress, CSR helps companies live up to their responsibilities as global citizens and local neighbors in a fast-changing world.

For Indian businesses CSR can be a source of opportunity, innovation, and competitive advantage while at the same time providing with the opportunity to actively contribute to the sustainable development. Organizations in India have been quite sensible in taking up CSR initiatives and integrating them in their business processes. It has become progressively projected in the Indian corporate setting because organizations have recognized that besides growing their businesses, it is also important to shape responsible and supportable relationships with the community at large. Business or corporate is a need of any country in order to grow its economy which will ultimately help the country to be a developed country. When we think of a business or corporation, their main aim is to earn profit and in order to earn a profit, they often practice some practices which may or may not be ethically correct. Hence in order to prevent the corporate from doing such activities government makes some laws as per the requirement of time and society.

While earning a profit, businesses are required to follow the law and even to make their policies customer-friendly and not exploitive for the customers or for the society. Businesses are required to do some work without expecting any benefits in order to serve society. The logic behind making businesses serve the society without any benefit is that the businesses use the social as well as natural resources in order to gain optimum utilization of their money and to get higher returns on their investments, hence the businesses should be more obliged to give something in return to the society without expecting any profit or benefit. This obligation of corporate to do something in favor of society at large without any benefit in return is known as Corporate Social Responsibility.Corporate Social Responsibility is practiced all over the globe as a voluntary activity in which the companies work for the society without expecting any profit in return. The acts are done for the benefit of society to help not only the society but also work in favor of the company's goodwill hence the work is not solely done for welfare purposes.

Corporate Social Responsibility in the global perspective is nothing new but when we talk about Corporate Social Responsibility from the Indian perspective, it has roots in India much before from the entry of any other external factors in India. We find evidence of the existence of Corporate Social Responsibility in the Scriptures from ancient times.

India has the world's richest tradition of Corporate Social Responsibility (CSR). The term CSR may be relatively new to India but the concept can be found in various documents of history and various religious books.

CHAPTER THREE

OBJECTIVES

To develop an understanding of concept of CSR

2. To analyze the development of CSR in India and its changing trends

3. To understand the policies governing CSR 4. To analyze the CSR initiatives in India including SMEs

4. To study the challenges faced by CSR in India

5. To provide suggestions for accelerating CSR initiatives

<u>**RESEARCH METHODOLOGY**</u>

The research paper is an attempt of exploratory research, based on the secondary data sourced from journals, magazines, articles, newspapers and media reports.

CSR

Defined most definitions describe CSR as a concept whereby companies integrate social and environmental concerns in their business operations and in their interaction with their stakeholders on a voluntary basis. (CEC: Green Paper for Promoting a European Framework for Corporate Social Responsibility) The World Business Council for Sustainable Development (WBCSD) defines CSR as "The continuing commitment by business to behave ethically and contribute to economic development while improving the quality of life of the work force and their families as well as of the local community and society at large". Kotler and Lee define CSR as "Corporate social responsibility is a commitment to improve community well-being through discretionary, business practices and contribution of corporate resources. Corporate social initiatives are major activities undertaken by a corporation to support social causes and to fulfill commitments to corporate social responsibility" Corporate social initiatives are major activities undertaken by a corporation to support social causes and to fulfill commitments to corporate social responsibility The conclusion would be that there is no unanimity on the definition of what constitutes Corporate

Social Responsibility (CSR).However what could be taken into account CSR is generally used to describe business's efforts to achieve sustainable outcomes by committing to good business practices and standards

Evolution of Corporate Social Responsibility: A Religious View

If we talk about the religions in India, then India is considered to be the most diverse country in the matters of religion and culture. Religion has a major role in the living styles of the people. Corporates working now or worked in any other time of history, have a sense of responsibility towards the society due to the religious interventions.

Followings indicate the existence of Corporate Social Responsibility in India much before the entry of Britishers or any other external forces.

- Vedas – There are four Vedas. Rig-Veda, Yajur-Veda, Sama-Veda, and Atharva -Veda. The prime component of these Vedas is the understanding of the concept of the universe. An attempt to help achieve one's goals and objective – i.e. union of self (atman) and the world (Brahma)
- Upanishads – Upanishads form the hardcore soul of the individual, laying a path to connect individual self to the supreme power, the God, and rise over and above the desire and liking from the materialistic pleasure.
- Bhagavad Gita – Krishna Gathas, the rhymes and preaching's Are the fundamental pillars establishing a sound base for spirituality and ethics, pronounced through a dialogue between Lord Krishna and the warrior Arjuna who is at a great crisis of his life? The karma yoga, Bhakti yoga and the notion of three Gunas (sattwa, Rajas, Tamas) have eminent implications in the context of ethical leadership, decision making, and management, the area of concern where the concepts of CSR Corporate Governance and ethics are expected to be practiced.
- Ramayana – It depicts the duties of relationships, portraying ideal characters like the ideal father, ideal servant, the ideal brother, the ideal wife and the ideal king. Apart from this, the Ramayana also teaches how the temptation for lust can bring a powerful and well-established man's doomsday.
- Buddhism – Lord Gautam Buddha gave the world with four fundamental noble truths. They are (i) Suffering exists; (ii) There is a cause of the suffering; (iii) Suffering can be eradicated; (iv) There is a means for the eradication of that suffering. His practice establishes the fact that

everything on earth is non–permanent and everything on earth has an – "anatta". Buddha also gave the world the eightfold path to liberation from all suffering.

- Islam had a law called Zakat, which rules that a portion of one's earning must be shared with the poor in the form of donations.

CHAPTER FOUR

CSR ORIGIN AND DEVELOPMENT IN INDIA

The concept of CSR has been imbibed in Indian society from the very beginning. Gandhi's philosophy of trusteeship is similar to CSR of the modern world; companies like TATA and BIRLA have been imbibing the case for social good in their operations for decades long before CSR become popular cause. The avid interest in community welfare among the Tata Group dates back to the 1860s when the company was founded by Jamshedji Tata. This explains why nearly two-thirds of the equity of Tata Sons, the Tata Group's promoter company, is held by philanthropic trusts, which have created a host of national institutions in science and technology, medical research, social studies and the performing arts. Dr.Kurien'sAmulled Operation flood had pioneered inclusive growth through work with dairy farmers at grass-root level, changing lives, enhancing income, empowering women and at the same time reaping benefits to the business.

At Indian Oil, corporate social responsibility (CSR) has been the cornerstone of success right from inception in the year 1964. The Corporation's objectives in this key performance area are enshrined in its Mission statement: "...to help enrich the quality of life of the community and preserve ecological balance and heritage through a strong environment conscience." Before Corporate Social Responsibility found a place in corporate lexicon, it was already textured into the Birla Group's value systems. As early as the 1940s, the founderi G.D Birla espoused the trusteeship concept of management. Simply stated, this entails that the wealth that one generates and holds is to be held as in a trust for our multiple stakeholders. With regard to CSR, this means investing part of our profits beyond business, for the larger good of society4 .Over the years CSR has gained importance in India as companies are realizing the importance of investing in CSR for achieving benefits of creating share holder value, increased revenue base, strategic branding, operational efficiency, better access to capital, human and intellectual capital and lower business risk.CSR has emerged as an effective tool that synergizes the efforts of Corporate and the social sector towards sustainable growth and development of societal objectives at large.

CHAPTER FIVE

CHANGING TRENDS IN CSR

FROM CHARITY TO RESPONSIBILITY An insight into the history of CSR reveals that till 1990s it was solely dominated by the idea of philanthropy. Considering CSR as an act of philanthropy, businesses often restricted themselves to one time financial grant and did not commit their resources for such projects. Moreover, businesses never kept the stakeholder in mind while planning for such initiatives, thereby reducing the efficacy and efficiency of CSR initiatives. However, over the last few years, the concept of CSR has been changing There has been an apparent transition from giving as an obligation or charity to giving as a strategy or responsibility.5 Review of the case studies and work done on CSR by companies in India suggests that the CSR is slowly moving away from charity and dependence and starting to build on empowerment and partnership.

CHAPTER SIX

MAKING A DIFFERENCE

CSR INITIATIVES IN INDIAN FIRMS Today, the corporate world has just started seeing the opportunity to help solve the problems CSR addresses. Private Sector has come out in favor of social responsibility and demonstrated their support for the Government's commitment to provide greater economic opportunities to the disadvantaged.

POLICY INITIATIVES

Realizing the role that can be played by corporate sector in addressing some of the glaring problems of a developing nation like India, ministry of corporate affairs (MCA) is expecting a fund flow of more than Rs 10,000 crore a year from private companies for social welfare initiatives as part of their CSR after Parliament clears the Companies Bill. Once the legislation is ratified by Parliament, India would become the first country to mandate CSR through a statutory provision. According to the proposal, it will be mandatory for private firms to earmark 2% of their average net profit for CSR initiatives. The government wants corporate houses to spend the sum in social sectors such as education and health rather than involving themselves in individual philanthropy6. MCA's draft voluntary guidelines on CSR are along global principles such as ethics and transparency, well-being of employees, human rights, health and safety, use of environment-friendly raw materials, following regulatory frameworks and larger engagement of stakeholders.

SOME EXAMPLES OF INDIAN CORPORATIONS' CSR ACTIVITIES
WELSPUN ENERGY LTD (WEL)

These Socially responsible and ethical business practices are the defining tenets of Welspun's corporate philosophy. ASSOCHAM has identified Welspun Energy with its CSR Excellence Award 2012. Welspun Energy Ltd is part of the $3.5 billion Welspun Group, which ranks amongst India's fastest emerging conglomerates with businesses in power generation, infrastructure, exploration and production of oil and natural gas, steel pipes and textiles CSR Programs By initiating programs like 'Training the Trainer', Enrolling children in Schools, 'Healthy Baby Competition' and Skill Development for Women, Welspun Energy has engaged with local communities to bring a positive change in their lives. Its social inclusion initiatives are beginning to show transformational results in Madhya Pradesh, Gujarat and Rajasthan. Welspun Energy's leadership is also involved in various forums which are focused on sustainable growth on a global scale; these are – B20's Green Growth Action Alliance, World Economic Forum's (WEF's) Steering Committee on Sustainable Infrastructure & Urban Development.

CHAPTER SEVEN

HUL (RURAL MARKETING)

HUL's CSR philosophy is embedded in its commitment to all stakeholders, including consumers and employees, the environment, and the society the company operates in. The company depends on sustainable sources of raw materials, and is committed to minimizing the environmental impact, improving sustainability throughout the value chain. Relating CSR to Business Strategies Product Development Water conserving products Human Resource Hiring and investing in local talent (merit-based through employment exchanges) Manufacturing Safety Health Environment Sourcing Code of Business Practices (COBP) Compliance Sales Shakti, cause marketing Investment Local enterprise development Profit apportionment Community involvement initiatives

Current Status of CSR in India

CSR activities performed by the corporate giants lacked specific guidelines about their measuring yardstick, investment parameters, areas to be covered for CSR activities, etc. With the span of time India became an opened economy from a closed economy, all due to the LPG movement launched in India in the year 1991. Since time immemorial CSR as a term lacked a precise definition, structure, criteria's and transparency. All Central Public Sector Enterprises (CPSE) were following the CSR guidelines issued by the Director of the Ministry of Heavy Industries and Public Enterprises since 2010. However the Companies Act, 2013 brought an end to the long wait by inserting Sec. 135 under the Companies Act 2013. The provisions under the Companies Act 2013 are as follows.

1. Every company having net worth of rupees five hundred crore or more, or turnover of rupees one thousand crore or more or a net profit of rupees five crore or more during any financial year shall constitute a Corporate Social Responsibility Committee of the Board consisting of

three or more directors, out of which at least one director shall be an independent director.

2. The Board's report under sub-section (3) of section 134 shall disclose the composition of the Corporate Social Responsibility Committee.

3. The Corporate Social Responsibility Committee shall,— (a) formulate and recommend to the Board, a Corporate Social Responsibility Policy which shall indicate the activities to be undertaken by the company as specified in Schedule VII; (b) recommend the amount of expenditure to be incurred on the activities referred to in clause (a), and (c) monitor the Corporate Social Responsibility Policy of the company from time to time.

4. The Board of every company referred to in subsection (1) shall,— (a) after taking into account the recommendations made by the Corporate Social Responsibility Committee, approve the Corporate Social Responsibility Policy for the Stakeholder Companies respond to the needs of stakeholders, customers, employees, communities, etc and disclose contents of such Policy in its report and also place it on the company's website, if any, in such manner as may be prescribed; and (b) ensure that the activities as are included in Corporate Social Responsibility Policy of the company are undertaken by the company.

5. The Board of every company referred to in subsection (1), shall ensure that the company spends, in every financial year, at least two percent. of the average net profits of the company made during the three immediately preceding financial years, in pursuance of its Corporate Social Responsibility Policy: Provided that the company shall give preference to the local area and areas around it where it operates, for spending the amount earmarked for Corporate Social Responsibility activities: Provided further that if the company fails to spend such amount, the Board shall, in its report made under clause (o) of sub-section (3) of section 134, specify the reasons for not spending the amount. Explanation – For the purposes of this section – "average net profit" shall be calculated in accordance with the provisions of section 198.

However, there still exist various issues and challenges in making the CSR activities to be performed successfully and due to which some amendments have been done in recent years as discussed below:

Corporate Social Responsibility (CSR): Under the Act, if companies that have to provide for CSR, do not fully spend the funds, they must disclose the reasons for non-spending in their annual report. Under the Bill, any unspent annual CSR funds must be transferred to one of the funds under Schedule 7 of the Act (e.g., PM Relief Fund) within six months of the financial year.

However, if the CSR funds are committed to certain ongoing projects, then the unspent funds will have to be transferred to an Unspent CSR Account within 30 days of the end of the financial year and spent within three years. Any funds remaining unspent after three years will have to be transferred to one of the funds under Schedule 7 of the Act. Any violation may attract a fine between Rs 50,000 and Rs 25,00,000 and every defaulting officer may be punished with imprisonment of up to three years or fine between Rs 50,000 and Rs 25,00,000, or both.

By keeping the implementation of Section 21 (amendments to the CSR provisions in Companies Act 2013) in abeyance, the government has restored status quo ante as regards CSR provisions, say company law experts.

This would mean that CSR, for now, would only be voluntary for corporate India and not spending the 2 percent on CSR would not be treated as a criminal offense, attracting jail term for company officials.

Environmental Protection and Corporate Social Responsibility

The environmental aspect of corporate responsibility of business organizations has been widely debated over the past decades as stakeholder's demands increase tremendously in organizations to be more socially responsible and environmentally conscious in their business operations. Porter & Kramer (2006) argued that social and environmental responsibility of organizations have become an inevitable priority for business leaders in every country, whereas Vogel (2006) maintained that neglecting environmental issues may be costly in the long run, and emphasized also on the impact that it can have on the legitimacy of the organization. Holtbrügge & Dögl (2012) wrote that there has been a significant change in global climate and environmental conditions, and argued that these changes have resulted in a growing public awareness of corporate environmental responsibilities (CER) as an important topic for both the business world and in academic literature. Other scholars have argued on the growing stakeholder's awareness and pressure on organizations concerning the pursuit of CER within their various fields.

CHAPTER EIGHT

SUGGESTION

· In order to ensure that CSR is progressively contributing and benefiting, the following suggestions are given to make CSR initiatives more effective

· It is found that there is a need for creation of awareness about CSR amongst the general public to make CSR initiatives more effective

· It is noted that partnerships between all stakeholders including the private sector, employees, local communities, the Government and society in general are either not effective or not effectively operational at the grassroots level in the CSR domain. It is recommended that appropriate steps be undertaken to address the issue of building effective bridges amongst all important stakeholders for the successful implementation of CSR initiatives. As a result, a long term and sustainable perspective on CSR activities should be built into the existing and future strategies of all stakeholders involved in CSR initiatives'

· The role of SME and their contribution to CSR in India has to be emphasized upon to increase their contribution to CS initiatives .When compared to large corporations, SME play a limited role in CSR.SME have to be encouraged to posivitely contribute and reap the benefits of created by CSR

· Allocating finance for treating CSR as an investment from which returns are expected

· Monitoring CSR activities and liaising closely with implementation partners such as NGOs to ensure that initiatives really deliver the desired outcomes

· A long term perspective by organisations, which encompasses their commitment to both internal and external stakeholders will be critical to the success of CSR and the ability of companies to deliver on the goals of their CSR strategy.

CHAPTER NINE

CONCLUSION

The concept of Corporate Social Responsibility is a very old concept as it has been discussed in all the historical documents and for a very long time, religion was the sole driver of encouraging people to carry on the activities for the welfare of society.

The history of Corporate Social Responsibility shows that the evolution of CSR in Indian history was done with subsequent development in the Indian Political and economic history. Further, it shows that the concept of Corporate Social Responsibility was a concept even when there was a codified law for governing the companies and to regulate various aspects of the management, the concept of Corporate Social Responsibility was not identified for many years and finally in 2013 law Corporate Social Responsibility was identified as law and under Section 135 of Companies Act, 2013 CSR was made obligatory on the corporate houses/ Companies.

In the amendment of 2019, it has been converted as a mandatory provision from an obligatory provision. The amendment has made non-usage of the CSR fund a Criminally punishable offense hence it is no longer an option of the companies but it is an obligation on the companies.

Corporate Social Responsibility has a part as Environmental Corporate Social Responsibility which contains the steps taken for the preservation of the environment by Corporate bodies and governments. Many corporate houses don't use Environmental concerns as Corporate responsibilities but they use it as a business marketing strategy in order to attract customers and to fulfill the obligations to save the environment and to meet with the criteria settled by the government to preserve the environment. CSR is really about ensuring that the company can grow on a sustainable basis, while ensuring fairness to all stakeholders, CSR has come a long way in India. It has successfully interwoven business with social inclusion and environment sustainability. From responsive activities to sustainable initiatives, corporate have clearly exhibited their ability to make a significant difference in the society and improve the overall quality of life. In the current social situation in India, it is difficult for one single entity to bring about change, as the scale is enormous. Corporate have the expertise, strategic thinking, manpower and money to facilitate extensive social change. Effective partnerships between corporate, NGOs and the government will place India's social development on a faster track.

www.ingramcontent.com/pod-product-compliance
Lightning Source LLC
Chambersburg PA
CBHW072146150726
48002CB00004B/1654